MAR 6 2020

MARK
MARKIPLIER
FISCHBACH
STAR YOUTUBE GAMER WITH 10 BILLION+ VIEWS

Philip Wolny

rosen publishing's
**rosen
central**

New York

Published in 2020 by The Rosen Publishing Group, Inc.
29 East 21st Street, New York, NY 10010

Library of Congress Cataloging-in-Publication Data

Names: Wolny, Philip, author.
Title: Mark "Markiplier" Fischbach: Star YouTube
Gamer with 10 Billion+ Views / Philip Wolny.
Description: First Edition. | New York: Rosen Central, 2020. | Series: Top video
gamers | Audience: Grades: 5–8. | Includes bibliographical references and index.
Identifiers: LCCN 2018047087| ISBN 9781725346048
(library bound) | ISBN 9781725346031 (paperback)
Subjects: LCSH: Markiplier—Juvenile literature. | Video
gamers—Biography—Juvenile literature.
Classification: LCC GV1469.3 .W955 2020 | DDC 794.8092 [B] —dc23
LC record available at https://lccn.loc.gov/2018047087

Manufactured in the United States of America

On the cover: YouTube personality, video gamer, and
comedian Mark Fischbach has expanded the boundaries of online
influence; he is shown here at a movie premiere in 2016.

CONTENTS

INTRODUCTION

It was March 2015, and Mark Edward Fischbach was in the hospital. He had undergone emergency surgery to remove a blockage from his intestine—leftover scar tissue from previous procedures. The event proved to not be serious, fortunately, but it was unusual for a twenty-six-year-old in otherwise good health. Fischbach's initial reaction was not that unusual, either: he decided to make a short video to remember the event. He asked the nurse to hold the camera while he gave an update on his health situation. What was unusual was that when he uploaded it to YouTube, the video got more than six million views.

While his driver's license might say Mark Fischbach, he is better known to the world by his online handle, Markiplier. He is an immensely popular YouTuber and gamer. The online star, who made his name with numerous Let's Play videos that make use of his oddball sense of humor, has more than twenty million subscribers on his YouTube channel.

In the hospital video, Markiplier has a tube up his nose. His voice is a hoarse whisper, a far cry from his normally rich baritone voice. Sometimes a little wild, and always funny and engaging, he has become one of the most influential pop culture figures of his generation. Among teenagers and gamers, he is one of the most popular and most watched content creators online.

Markiplier and some of his YouTuber and gamer peers are the pop stars for a new generation. It is a generation that is always online, and online fame can be short lived. Viral stars can explode on to the scene and seemingly fade away by the weekend. In this uncertain environment, it takes a certain type of unique star power to gain the kind of fame Markiplier has and not only maintain it—but grow it.

He and others in his circles are redefining entertainment and popularity itself. They are proving that it is no longer necessary to appear on a popular television show, have a hit on the pop charts, or shoot a monster jump shot in basketball to have an impact on millions of dedicated fans. In 2015, Susanne Ault of *Variety*

Mark "Markiplier" Fischbach signs autographs at Comic-Con in San Diego, California, in July 2016. He never imagined gaming would earn him the celebrity and fan following he now has.

magazine noted that "eight of the top 10 slots in a survey ranking talent … are now commanded by YouTube creators." While pop stars and athletes of the past became extremely popular for being different (more artistic, more athletic) from the average fan, Markiplier and other online personalities are not quite like this. Much of their popularity comes from being approachable, everyday—but still very talented—people, who just happen to also be gamers.

Markiplier has also never been afraid of trying new things or experimenting with new formats. He has more recently started to branch out into comedy. Despite setbacks, personal losses—including friends and family—and the difficulties of being a career online entertainer, Markiplier continues to thrive.

CHAPTER 1

Before There Was Markiplier ...

In the 1980s, Mark's father, a career US Army soldier, met his mother in South Korea. They later moved around a bit before settling in Hawaii. In 1987, they welcomed their first child into the world: Jason Thomas Fischbach, called Thomas. On June 28, 1989, Mark Edward was born at Tripler Army Medical Center on the island of O'ahu in the state capital, Honolulu. He was a big baby at 10 pounds and 3 ounces (4.6 kilograms).

An Ideal Childhood

Not long after Mark was born, his father retired from the military after twenty-three years. They moved all the way to Cincinnati, Ohio, where Mark's father would work as an illustrator in publishing. The boys spent their early years there.

In a video series titled "Draw My Life," Mark described his family's time growing up in Cincinnati as an ideal childhood, adventurous and fun:

> We moved into this awesome home with a gigantic backyard that led into these really amazing woods where me and my brother spent most of our time. I mean, if we weren't on the computer, we were out in the woods playing in the creek,

picking up tadpoles, cutting vines, swinging on them. I mean, we really bonded together over those woods and that's one of the things that I miss most about that house.

When not outside, the brothers spent time on the computer. Mark credits his father with introducing the boys to computers very early. "I mean, seriously, this thing blew my mind at the time because I could not imagine ever living without out it," he said in "Draw My Life."

The brothers also fell in love with video games. It was the 1990s, and computer games had been around for some time. However, the era's gaming consoles were a far cry from the simple, seemingly primitive computer graphics of early 1980s arcade classics, such as *Pac-Man* or *Donkey Kong*. Newer, more advanced systems took video games to another level: from a child's hobby to a multibillion-dollar industry. Like their backyard adventures, gaming introduced the boys to a world of imagination before the internet truly took center stage.

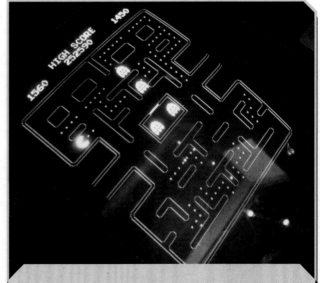

Computer software generally, and game technology in particular, has come a long way since an earlier generation became obsessed with arcade games like *Pac-Man*, which launched in 1980.

Divorce: Ups and Downs

The boys especially bonded over the Super Nintendo console that Thomas got one Christmas. Mark said on "Draw My Life," "This thing was the reason that me and my brother are so close today, because we played so many games together with it." Brotherly bonding soon became even more important. While it had seemed like an ideal life, Mark and Thomas's parents fought fairly frequently. Mark thought his mother in particular was unhappy with the marriage, especially

Gaming consoles from the 1990s, such as the Super Nintendo pictured here, excited youths like the Fischbach brothers with their more advanced graphics and playability.

since their father was a good deal older than her. They mostly tried to ignore it, and their parents tried to patch things up.

Eventually, however, divorce became inevitable. Financially, their two-income household split. With the boys staying with their father more of the time, there was less money for video games or pretty much anything else. Mark had gone to private school but had to transfer to the local public school to save money. The big house Mark loved so much had to be sold, too. Luckily, the boys kept their computer and console. Mark felt greater stress from seeing his father fall into a deep depression after the divorce than he did by their changed circumstances.

New Beginnings

In addition to the tough divorce, other changes and challenges loomed. Among of these were adjusting to losing old friends and having to make new ones; Mark even had to get used to lockers in public school, which he had never before encountered. For someone whose sometimes-outrageous exploits would later earn him fame, it was only natural that Mark would make friends by doing something dumb and dangerous.

As kids sometimes do, Mark and his friends were having a contest to see how far they could jump off some playground monkey bars. Mark expected victory, but he soon realized just how bad an idea it had really been: He hit the ground and broke two bones in his arm. He had to wear a cast for a while. A fellow student named Drew started helping Mark out with tasks he could not easily do alone, including sharpening pencils. Drew also convinced Mark to join in the school band, where he got into playing trumpet. Slowly but steadily, Mark eased into a normal school life and adjusted to his parents' divorce. He even started dating.

His father's situation improved. The elder Fischbach started dating, eventually meeting a woman named Dee. Mark described her on "Draw My Life" as "pretty much the nicest person that we ever met." It did not hurt that Dee knew her new boyfriend's sons well enough to buy them a PlayStation 2 as a present. They appreciated that, but Mark more appreciated the fact that she made his father happy. Things were looking up.

At one point, Markiplier was intrigued by what made video games click behind the scenes, which sparked an interest in coding or programming. However, he ultimately decided to study engineering.

Life Goals and Loss

Mark's life entered a comfortable groove. Like any typical teenager, he was weighing his options and debating future plans. He blew off steam by playing *Half-Life 2* and other popular games. Things finally seemed straightforward and simple—a rare thing for many teens just getting their bearings in life. He was toying with the idea of studying computer science, with the intention of becoming a video game developer.

His father pulled him aside one day to show him a piece of paper. Mark read it silently. His dad had cancer, and it looked to be terminal. He only had a short while to live. Few other events in his life devastated Mark like his father's diagnosis. Confronting the emotional anxiety caused by his father's illness made Mark lose his sense of direction. Instead of a concrete plan for the future, he was now drifting, unsure of what paths he should follow.

Mark's father ended up living longer than doctors expected, but his condition worsened. Meanwhile, the ordeal had Mark flip-flopping on his future. He had settled on engineering as a career path but still had doubts. He switched from civil engineering to biomedical engineering and then back again. The idea of making games for a living was also calling to him as he began his studies at the University of Cincinnati (UC).

Mark was nineteen, with a year of college behind him, when he woke up one summer day to commotion. Dee (now his stepmother) was screaming. The boys rushed downstairs to meet the moment they had awaited but hoped would never come: their father was dying.

At this point, things really seemed to speed up and get even more confusing and painful for Mark. He felt stuck in engineering, especially, and in a rut generally. Neither his studies nor his first few jobs were satisfying to him.

CHAPTER 2

From Hobby to Career

Around the time that Fischbach started at UC, the online video streaming and video sharing platform known as YouTube was only a few years old. It had officially launched in February 2005. Google bought the service in 2006, seeing its enormous potential. It has only grown in reach and influence since, becoming as important for creators and businesses in many industries as television and radio once were. One minute, someone can watch an epic fail video of someone falling into a swimming pool—the next, a serious political discussion at a book release party, and then a music video from his or her favorite artist. Anyone visiting the site or uploading videos themselves knows the possibilities are endless.

Pushing the Envelope Online

In addition, a new generation of young people were taking the free or relatively cheap tools on YouTube and other networks to transform the internet in their own image. These digital natives—including Markiplier—had little memory of a life before everyone was seemingly online. YouTubers have created their own cultures, fandoms, and communities. Gaming became one of the largest entertainment sectors, and a major part of geek culture, alongside comics, animation, Japanese anime, and many other interests. Gamers also became an economic force to reckon with. Kellie Ell of CNBC reported that the video game market will have grown to a staggering $138 billion by the end of 2018.

Older generations produced television shows reviewing films or covering theater and other art forms. Younger people naturally created content about one of their favorite things: video games.

Launched in February 2005, YouTube quickly became an online phenomenon. Markiplier and others from his generation would invent hundreds of new ways to entertain and profit using the site.

Enter Mark Fischbach, gamer and engineering major. He was unhappy for reasons beyond his father's death. His typical office jobs, where he was doing work he was not passionate about, were bringing his spirits down. He needed something else.

Markiplier Is Born

Soon enough, Fischbach decided to leave college, putting engineering behind him for good. He also was dying to leave standard office jobs and break out into something more exciting. He even worked as a bartender and carpenter occasionally. At one point, a medical emergency landed him in the hospital. A constant pain in his side was revealed to be his appendix, which had swelled up dangerously and needed to be removed. Doctors also noted a fist-sized tumor in his adrenal gland that would have to come out much later.

After his hospital ordeal, he bought a video camera to use for YouTube videos. In March 2012, Fischbach joined YouTube with his first channel, called Markiplier. On April 4, 2012, he began his YouTube gaming career with a playthrough video of the horror game *Amnesia: The Dark Descent*. Horror games have consistently been among Fischbach's favorites to play, review, and create other content around.

A devoted and serious gamer, Fischbach was also a natural in front of the camera. His first videos were mostly game walkthroughs. Walkthroughs have been a major part of gamer culture for a long time. They are one of several kinds of gaming-related YouTube content that has sprung up in recent years. Some of the major types of gaming videos on YouTube can be categorized as follows:

Markiplier made a name for himself by playing survival horror games, starting with *Amnesia: The Dark Descent*. His dramatic reactions to these games are what helped make him famous.

- **Let's Play:** Someone plays a game with a running commentary. These are edited to maintain a fast pace and are meant to keep viewers engaged and amused, rather than work as instructional videos.
- **Playthrough:** This is when someone films himself or herself playing through an entire game. There are few edits or transitions in many of these videos. Sometimes, the terms playthrough and Let's Play are used interchangeably, but Let's Play videos do not necessarily show the entire game being played.
- **Walkthrough:** The player provides concise instructions on how to make it through a game, or sometimes just one level or part of the game. These videos are used to help other players and to point out fun hidden objectives, items, or locations, among other goals.

A Phoenix from the Ashes

YouTube's business is based on advertising. Most people are used to having to watch a brief advertisement before many YouTube videos. Such ads, running on YouTube itself and embedded on millions of other sites, allow users to make a tiny bit of money every time someone watches at least part or all of an ad. However, when Fischbach started on YouTube, this system, known as AdSense, could be notoriously uncertain. Many account holders who made some—or all—of their living creating videos complained about seemingly arbitrary, random rules and reasons why they were suddenly penalized by the system.

In May 2012, Fischbach butted heads with YouTube, which disabled his AdSense account. He appealed the decision but lost. Soon after, as he revealed in one of his last videos on the original Markiplier channel, he had to set up a new one, MarkiplierGAME, to continue to make videos and earn money. Fischbach felt optimistic and inspired because he had a few thousand views for many of the earlier videos he had posted; this was more views, even, than he had followers, which he believed was a great sign of growing popularity.

Entertainers from older media, such as television and the music industry, were often far removed from fans. YouTube popularity and success, however, is based on connections between content creators and fans. Fischbach did a walkthrough or a playthrough almost daily, communicating with his fans all the while.

He had amazing growth in 2012, his first year on his new channel. By the end of the year, he hit fifty thousand subscribers. Earlier, he had begun a tradition of posting a video to celebrate new milestones in subscriber numbers. From four thousand in August, he hit twenty-five thousand in October, before reaching fifty thousand in late December.

Not Just a Game

Reborn now as Markiplier, the young creator was doing it all via trial and error, while getting his own advice from friends, novices, and veterans alike. It became clear that he was doing something he loved, despite the hard work. Some people might watch his

Sound Advice

In a forum post on the r/letsplay sub-Reddit in December 2012, Markiplier looked back at a year of constant YouTubing. He admitted he was amazed by the engagement he felt with his growing fan base. With some experience now under his belt, he had some practical advice for others starting their own channels. In his own words, he advised the following:

In addition to YouTube, many gamers and other content creators and personalities make use of a variety of platforms to communicate with fans, including Reddit.

- "Above all else, you have to enjoy what you're doing ... I worked incredibly hard (12 hours a day) trying to get attention for my channel. I enjoyed it so much that I sprang out of bed in the morning and lost sleep at night."

- He strongly advised budding YouTubers to "exhaustively connect with your audience. If you have a single person that truly enjoys your videos and messages you, you have to engage them personally. They are your champion early on and you need to make sure that they feel like it." Fischbach pointed out that the most lasting promotion was word of mouth.

- "The hardest truth to understand is that even if your content is the best in the world, no one is looking for it," he warned novice creators. The burden is on creators to make it as easy as possible for others to discover their content. After all, it can be hard for a potential viewer to sift through an ocean of videos and posts.

With his typical humor and fanfare, Markiplier is shown here striking a pose at the October 2016 Streamy Awards, where he was nominated in the gaming category.

videos or those of fellow gaming personalities, such as Evan Fong (aka VanossGaming) or Alia "Lia" Shelesh (aka SSSniperWolf), and conclude that it is the easiest and best job in the world. Who would not want to play video games for a living? This is an oversimplification, however. Markiplier and others put hours and hours of work into conceiving, producing, and promoting their content.

YouTube has made it possible for good gamers with personality to become small businesspeople in their own right. Markiplier puts all of his talents to use, including his gaming skills and his sense of humor and creativity, to put on a good show. His promotional efforts, viewer-milestone videos, and other in-jokes and background all contribute to great fan response.

As the MarkiplierGAME channel grew, advertisers and companies took notice of the power of YouTube's new celebrities. In 2015, *Variety*'s Susanne Ault reported, "Teens' emotional attachment to YouTube stars is as much as seven times greater than that toward a traditional celebrity; and YouTube stars are perceived as seventeen times more engaging, and eleven times more extraordinary, than mainstream stars." In that same article, Markiplier was listed as the sixth most influential entertainer among teens, ahead of even pop stars Bruno Mars and Taylor Swift.

CHAPTER 3

Moving on Up

I n June 2013, Markiplier was riding high. On June 16, he released his 500,000 subscriber milestone video. In the video notes, he again thanked his fans for all their support during his incredible (and admittedly unlikely) journey from confused college student to rising online star.

Finding a Groove

Markiplier became a seasoned YouTube veteran, finding his groove and distinguishing himself in a very crowded field. He uses both his smooth voice and his face very creatively, especially in his own witty takes on reaction videos. Reaction videos—in which a YouTuber films himself or herself reacting to a real event, movie trailer, video game, or nearly any other bit of content—have become extremely popular in recent years.

In a playthrough video, Markiplier might insert snippets of other media, such as GIFs, movie clips, Vines, or other content, to show his reaction to especially frightening parts and to underscore the feelings he had while playing the game. Early on, he spiced up his videos by using his face camera to broadcast his reactions into a corner of the video. The first face cam playthrough he posted was for *Amnesia: The Dark Descent*, back in April 2012.

Wilford Warfstache and Other Characters

His dedicated fans know about Markiplier's longtime interest in comedy. The first sketch comedy video he posted was titled "The Fall of Slender Man," uploaded in November 2012. It was a spoof on the eerie and popular urban legend about a monstrous character that was created on the web horror fiction site Creepypasta. In this video, Markiplier first introduced the outlandish character known as Wilford Warfstache.

The character is a pink bowtie–wearing journalist with Markiplier's trademark curled pink plastic mustache. Warfstache has a funny, exaggerated voice. This character's personality is over the top, a little

Far more than just a talking head, Markiplier's fans are drawn in by his character work, sketches, and the other ways he distinguishes himself from the YouTube pack.

silly, and quick to anger—but in a comical way. Warfstache has been among his most popular and longest-running characters.

Another character is an emotionally darker version of himself, named Darkiplier, whose negativity contrasts with his own typically sunny personality. Markiplier has also frequently performed a recurring version of Santa Claus in a series of videos. His Santa, however, is mean to his elves and can occasionally drink too much eggnog. Other lesser-known characters include Mark-Bot (a robot version of Mark himself) and a version of Shane Walsh, a long-dead villain from an early season of the popular show *The Walking Dead*.

His emotional responses to events in a game, including yelling and sometimes even bursting into tears, also made fans take notice. Besides merely discussing the games themselves, he often posts vlogs about gaming, the industry, and many other topics. Because of his warm and sensitive approach, Markiplier fans feel like he is talking directly to them. Meanwhile, his emotional vulnerability is often on display. Many other gamer stars online do not wear their hearts on their sleeves as Markiplier does.

Hello, Hollywood!

In 2014, Fischbach moved to Los Angeles, California. Living there offered him the chance to meet and collaborate with many other YouTubers, comedians, and creative thinkers, including fellow online gamers. The possibilities were endless.

Despite their growing market share, many people still dismissed games as child's play, an opinion that Markiplier found unfortunate. He hoped to change people's minds and to gain some respect for his fans, himself, and his friends.

With his characteristic flair, he was able to do just that when opportunity presented itself. Late-night television show host Jimmy Kimmel suffered a backlash from the gaming community when he said publicly that he could not imagine why other people would want to watch strangers play video games on YouTube. He even received death threats from some gamers who lashed out inappropriately.

To make peace, Kimmel invited Markiplier and fellow YouTube gamer star Jonna Mae, known to fans primarily as MissesMae, to appear on *Jimmy Kimmel Live!* Patricia Hernandez of the gaming and culture site Kotaku.com reported that Mae and Markiplier tried to convert Kimmel in a good-natured way. When explaining the appeal of Let's Play content, Markiplier explained, "I love watching other people have fun, and I think that's what a lot of people get out of it." When Kimmel joked that everyone wanted to kill him, Markiplier replied, "Not everyone. I'm pretty sure mostly people want you to understand." Ultimately, while Kimmel did not turn into an avid gamer, he left the show that night more enlightened about a passion that inspires and entertains millions worldwide.

Even someone as sarcastic and skeptical as late-night television talk show host Jimmy Kimmel seemed to warm up to gaming with help from Markiplier and Jonna "MissesMae" Mae.

It Takes a Community

Being constantly online can be isolating, but it also connects millions of digital citizens in unexpected ways. Gamers like to play with others online and together with their friends in person. Playthroughs and other game videos can feel very one-on-one, too. Markiplier and his peers will often reject the notion that gaming makes you lonely and depressed. However, playing too much and too often is unhealthy.

In the early 2010s, the MarkiplierGAME community was growing. This meant that Markiplier had to engage with his fans more than ever and collaborate with other stars to make interesting new content. He worked with Cyndago, an online sketch comedy team made up of Ryan Magee and Daniel Kyre (later with help from friend Matt Watson), to post their first video together in February 2013, titled "Danger in Fiction."

By late 2013, Fischbach had hit the incredible subscriber milestone of one million. With his earnings, he helped fly the Cyndago team out to Los Angeles for a week. All of them decided to move there permanently. Their dark and bizarre satires were a great fit for Fischbach, and they let him express himself beyond gaming. The relationship not only made fast friends of Fischbach and the team, but it was also great for synergy—that is, Fischbach and Cyndago were able to gain new fans from each other and each was able to branch out creatively. Plus, the guys all became roommates, making it even easier to work and blow off steam together.

Monetizing MarkiplierGAME

Like everyone else on YouTube, Markiplier makes most of his money through AdSense. YouTube creators have to decide exactly what kinds of ads they want attached to their videos and even which videos to make money from, or monetize. Some of the main kinds of ads are:

- **Display ads:** These visuals run alongside a video but not over it or on it, making them one of the least invasive types of ads.
- **Overlay ads:** These banner ads appear at the bottom of the screen where content is played. These are still relatively unintrusive.
- **Unskippable video ads:** These ads are usually up to thirty seconds long, and users cannot click or skip ahead but must let them play through. These ads offer the most compensation for a channel since they put potential customer eyes on inescapable snippets of advertising. Many new creators tend to avoid these, though, especially if they are just starting out and want new fans to easily engage with their material without ads discouraging them.
- **Bumper ads:** These are also unskippable, but usually are only several seconds long, making them still profitable but less annoying. Content creators afraid of scaring off new fans can rest easy with these.
- **Skippable video ads:** These videos play for a few seconds or more until a "Skip Ad" button appears, which

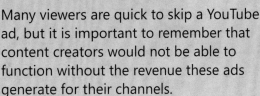

Many viewers are quick to skip a YouTube ad, but it is important to remember that content creators would not be able to function without the revenue these ads generate for their channels.

Triumph and Tragedy

In many ways, 2015 was a breakthrough year for Markiplier. In the video announcing that his channel had reached eight million subscribers, he broke down and thanked his fans yet again. The video showed split-screens of him and many different fans all crying together and got eleven million views. His sincerity and gratitude shone through yet again, underscoring that his fans' dedication and support were appreciated and reciprocated, no matter how big his channel got. In addition, members of the Markiplier community sounded off in the video's comments, offering each other help and support for those who revealed problems and difficulties they were experiencing.

Even as his popularity grew, though, tragedy struck. On September 19, Ryan Magee of Cyndago revealed that Daniel Kyre had been rushed to the hospital. He had attempted suicide. Despite all medical efforts to revive him, he suffered permanent and severe brain damage. Kyre was taken off life support on September 18, 2015.

Kyre's death crushed Markiplier, hurting him more than anything had since his father's death. He needed time off to process the event, heal, and help his friends, roommates, and collaborators do likewise. It was a major event for his fans, too, who felt his pain. He had barely missed a day of uploading since 2012. A visibly shaken Markiplier posted on September 21, explaining what had happened to his fans in a highly emotional video filmed in Cincinnati, Ohio, where he had gone to deal with the pain. Cyndago dissolved their team but would reform later with other partners and under new names. Fischbach lost not just a friend, but also someone who challenged him to improve his game, learn new aspects of video production, and much more.

allows users to do just that. These types of ads are extremely common.

- **Sponsored cards:** Viewers are shown a teaser for an ad for a few seconds, which they can click on, or select an icon in the video's top right section to browse. These are typically products or services related to the content of the video.

A fan takes a selfie with Markiplier at the 2016 San Diego Comic-Con. Fan engagement is one major way that YouTube stars distinguish themselves from the other celebrities and creators.

How much does Markiplier make from his videos? A notorious crew of hackers based in Saudi Arabia—called OurMine—infiltrated his YouTube account in late 2015. They did not steal any money or any personal details, but they did reveal that in November 2015, Markiplier made $665,820, according to Bill Roberts of Vlogger Gear. If that was an average monthly income, he made as much as $8 million that year. Even with money going to his producers and other support staff, it is obvious that a gaming YouTube channel is far from child's play.

CHAPTER 4

Top of the World

Things were now moving fast. By October 2015, MarkiplierGAME had ten million subscribers. By the end of the year, it was at eleven million. Markiplier was slowly edging out the competition. In June 2017, *Forbes* reported that Markiplier had become gaming's most influential YouTuber, surpassing not just PewDiePie, but also Mark's own sometime collaborator JackSepticEye, as well as VanossGaming, OMGItsfirefoxx, and other big names.

Markiplier's popularity has even challenged that of Swedish gamer and fellow YouTuber PewDiePie, who has the most popular channel of all time, despite his controversial actions.

Rolling with the Punches

Change is inevitable with rising popularity and financial success. A YouTuber's community will be far different at ten thousand subscribers than at ten million. Some popular YouTubers have drawn controversy for offensive or inappropriate behavior—

including PewDiePie and Logan Paul, two of the site's biggest names. Markiplier, however, has managed to stay grounded while building his own niche.

Markiplier told Julia Alexander of Polygon.com in early 2018 that he hoped to be an example: someone who was helping to build a caring and engaged community around gaming and sketch comedy,

Livestreaming and Giving Back

Markiplier is committed to helping others in the best way he knows how: gaming. Almost monthly, Markiplier holds an hours-long livestream of a playthrough that doubles as an online funding drive for a specific cause or charity organization. His first two were in October 2012 for Living Beyond Breast Cancer. He has livestreamed to support organ donorship, research cures for Alzheimer's disease, to promote tolerance and LGBTQ causes, and for children's hospitals, including St. Jude's Children's Research Hospital and Cincinnati Children's Hospital. One particularly important cause for Fischbach was helping out the Depression and Bipolar Support Alliance to the tune of $276,000. His motivations included his own periodic depression, helping others, and honoring the memory of his dear friend Daniel Kyre.

In November 2017, Fischbach hosted a livestream with his friends Ethan and Tyler, during which they played the games Cards Against Humanity and Jenga. They quickly surpassed the fundraising goal of $200,000, which they later donated to the relief organization Save the Children. They eventually raised an incredible $422,000. Fischbach declared via Twitter that it was "bigger than anything we've ever done before." In total, throughout his YouTube career, Markiplier has raised more than $3 million for the various charities he has promoted.

rather than starting online fights like a troll. Asked about how the public might see Paul and others' behavior, he said, "I'm afraid they'll think YouTubers are only these dancing monkeys that don't take things seriously ... We're not all reckless ... There's a huge group of YouTubers that take things extremely seriously and try to approach things with the utmost professionalism."

This has helped distinguish Markiplier and some of his friends from clickbait vloggers who are only in it for the money and care little about their fans or are likely to fade and disappear amid scandals. For Markiplier, his YouTube community is a home that needs to be cared for and respected.

Another issue facing many YouTubers is burning out. As with any job, YouTubing can become monotonous, repetitive, and even creatively exhausting. It happened to Markiplier in 2017, when he announced a one-month hiatus. "When you're doing the same grind for six years, it will get anybody down," he told Alexander of Polygon.com. He added, "I wasn't upset with how much work I was doing, but I was upset with doing so much work and I wasn't proud of what I was making. I had to step back and reevaluate what I was doing and where I was coming from."

Putting in Overtime

Markiplier's channel depends on constant promotional work. This includes doing tours, negotiating deals with software vendors and game makers, and making appearances at conventions, or cons, and other conferences and meet-ups. He will often speak at cons—sometimes on panels about games or other pop culture topics—and do meet and greets with fans, take pictures, and listen intently to their stories. Some of the biggest events he regularly attends are the various Comic Cons that take place nationwide, the South by Southwest (SXSW) new music and interactive media festival in Austin, Texas, and PAX (once called the Penny Arcade Expo), a series of events for gamers to play games and meet with each other.

While his Let's Play videos remain a big part of his life, he has slowly transitioned to doing more comedy sketches, which have always been a passion for him. In fact, before gaming launched him to fame and fortune, he toyed with the idea of being a standup or an improv comic, as well as a voice actor.

Markiplier frequently makes public appearances at conventions and shows across the world. He is shown here contributing as a panel member at PAX, a popular gaming convention.

In September 2017, Markiplier announced that he was going on tour. After a four-show stand in the United States that June, Markiplier joined LordMinion777, Tyler Scheid, and CrankGameplays to visit various US and European cities. Called the You're Welcome

Tour, the show had more than thirty stops. Each performance was unique, though the bulk of the show was built around a mixture of sketch comedy and musical theater.

Live shows allow Markiplier to connect even more closely with his fans, especially those who might live in remote areas. They also help him sharpen his skills and reflexes and make him happy because they let him express himself creatively in ways that gaming online all the time might not. It was exciting, too, to work as part of a larger comedy troupe, since Markiplier typically collaborates with a much smaller team. The You're Welcome Tour marched on to Australia in November 2018.

What Comes Next?

Despite the wide and varied success Markiplier has experienced, his life has also been marked by terrible events. Tragedy struck yet again in early 2018 when he again had to step away from his YouTube duties to mourn his nineteen-year old niece, Miranda, who died in a car accident. Miranda had been one of his earliest supporters, as he often pointed out. He set up a page on the GoFundMe crowdfunding website to help her family with funeral costs. The initial goal of $15,000 was soon shattered—fans donated almost $75,000. Markiplier also announced that he would again take a break from YouTubing.

In the late 2010s, Markiplier is in a good place—and not just in his career. He is in a long-term relationship with his girlfriend, Amy Nelson (also known as Peebles). Like Fischbach, she hails from Cincinnati and moved to Los Angeles, where she works in graphic

Markiplier: Quick-Hit Facts

- He is known for frequently changing his hair color and has dyed his hair blue, black, red, pink, and other colors.
- Markiplier says he suffers from automatonophobia, which is a fear of mannequins and similar dolls and figures.
- He has visited his mother's native country, Korea, on three separate occasions.
- On a livestream, Markiplier once told fans that he had been diagnosed with mild attention deficit hyperactivity disorder (ADHD).
- Two of Fischbach's favorite phrases while vlogging are "but either way ..." and "well, alright then."
- Markiplier's famous logo—a digital letter *M* with his trademark pink mustache—is all over his creative content. It is also featured on the hoodies, dog leashes, t-shirts, coffee cups, and other merchandise fans can buy on his online shop.
- A few of his close collaborators are his friends Tyler Scheid, Wade Barnes, Bob Muyskens, and Ethan Nestor-Darling. Scheid serves as Markiplier's manager. Other frequent creative partners include PewDiePie and JackSepticeye, a fellow Let's Play veteran, comedian, and performer.

design and animation. Nelson also makes guest appearances in his videos and was a fan of his channel before they met at an industry event.

As one of YouTube's brightest stars, Markiplier looks forward to what comes next. He plans to continue concentrating more and more on sketch comedy, touring, and trying his hand at a musical

Markiplier and a friend are shown here at a reception for Streamy Award nominees at YouTube Space LA in 2016. Such events are yet another common stop on a popular YouTuber's schedule.

career as well. His creative journey has inspired him to follow many of his dreams, even if he does not do them all at once. He decided to take lessons from vocal coaches and enjoys both singing and songwriting.

Meanwhile, he tries to stay humble while also dealing with just how big the Markiplier community has become. He knows his millions of fans and the world at large are watching closely, and he especially does not want to disappoint those fans, as he hopes to grow and learn and may not always be a YouTube gamer first and foremost. Most of all, he hopes to keep improving and making quality work. As he told Julie Alexander of Polygon.com in 2018:

> I'm not the best at what I do yet, but I'm always going to work harder to find something that I'm passionate about, something that I could gain some confidence from. When it comes down to the future, I simply look at new opportunities as new ways that I can invent myself, new ways that I can approach YouTube. If it's innovative, that's good. If it's reenergizing, that's good. If it's just something that makes me happy, well, that's really good.

Regardless of what he does, Markiplier has continued to welcome legions of fans into his community, where they have been entertained, comforted, and made to feel at home. Whatever the future holds for him, he vows to keep working hard, expanding his horizons, and making his young fans laugh, cry, think, and enjoy themselves.

1989 Mark Edward Fischbach, the future Markiplier, is born at Tripler Army Medical Center in O'ahu, Hawaii, on June 28.

2008 Mark's father passes away from cancer, leaving his sons devastated.

2012 Fischbach buys a camera and sets up his first YouTube channel to post videos under the name Markiplier.

He is forced to abandon his first channel due to issues with YouTube's AdSense program and launches MarkiplierGAME, dedicated to video game playthroughs and other related content.

He builds an audience from a handful of followers to fifty thousand subscribers.

2013 MarkiplierGAME surpasses half a million subscribers in June.

Markiplier and Cyndago collaborate on their very first comedy video.

Toward the end of the year, Markiplier's channel hits one million subscribers.

2014 *Variety* declares Markiplier to be one of the most influential stars among teenagers.

2015 Markiplier surpasses eight million subscribers, celebrating and announcing the achievement in an epic, emotional video in which he and his fans cry and rejoice.

Markiplier mourns the death of one of his best friends and collaborators, Daniel Kyre of the Cyndago video team, and takes a break from YouTubing.

Markiplier is hacked by the OurMine hacker collective, but luckily not much is revealed or stolen.

Markiplier officially hits ten million subscribers.

2017 *Forbes* declares Markiplier the most influential gaming YouTuber, taking the title from sometime collaborator PewDiePie.

Markiplier takes a short hiatus to avoid burning out from overwork and creative exhaustion.

Alongside other YouTubers, Markiplier announces a major tour that will eventually hit many US cities, Europe, and other destinations.

2018 Markiplier mourns another loss in his life when a beloved niece, Miranda, is killed in a car accident. He again takes a leave of absence to mourn and regroup.

GLOSSARY

baritone Describing a moderately deep voice, typically male.

bumper ads Relatively short ads on YouTube that cannot be skipped.

channel On YouTube, this is the home page for a user's account and may be used either recreationally or as a way to make money.

crowdfunding A modern way of raising money by appealing to as many people as possible via online platforms.

display ad An ad that runs alongside a video but does not interfere with playback or presentation.

embedded Refers to video or other content that originates on one site but can be displayed on another or played on another.

geek culture A subculture of people enthusiastic about certain areas of pop culture, including ones related to gaming, comics, and technology.

handle The name of someone's social media account on an internet platform, like YouTube, Twitter, Instagram, and others.

improv A type of comedy entertainment in which the participants make up a script and act it out in real time, without prior preparation or writing.

influencer A person famous on social media who is considered influential to his or her fans or followers, often sought after by marketers to help sell products.

Let's Play A type of YouTube video that became popular in the 2010s, in which the player records or recounts playing a video game with commentary running over it.

livestream A real-time video or live transmission of an event online; or, the act of doing such a stream.

monetization The process of earning money for one's services and especially one's content online, such as YouTube videos.

overlay ad A kind of ad that appears at the bottom of a video that is streaming.

playthrough A video of a whole game being played from start to finish.

synergy In marketing and promotion, when two things or entities are combined to benefit both parties.

vlogging Short for "video blogging," vlogging includes posting videos regularly on any conceivable subject.

walkthrough A video made for the purpose of instructing others on how to pass certain levels of, or successfully complete, a game.

Children's Safety Association of Canada
2110 Kipling Avenue
PO Box 551
Etobicoke, ON M9W 4KO
Canada
(888) 499-4444
Website: http://www.safekid.org/en
The Children's Safety Association of Canada promotes health and safety among children across Canada, with recent programs emphasizing online safety, the threats of cyberbullying, and other modern issues.

Digital Media Association
1050 17th Street NW, Suite 220
Washington, DC 20036
(202) 792-5274
Email: info@dima.org
Website: http://www.dima.org
Twitter: @digitalmediausa
The Digital Media Association is an advocacy group for digital media professionals, including webcasters, technologists, and others who make their living online.

EA Vancouver
4330 Sanderson Way
Burnaby, BC V5G 4X1
Canada
(604) 456-3600
Website: https://www.ea.com/en-ca

Facebook, Instagram, and Twitter: @ea

EA Vancouver is the Canadian base for Electronic Arts, the second-largest gaming company in Europe and the Americas. Its Vancouver headquarters is its largest and oldest branch, having formerly been a separate Canadian company called Distinctive Software, founded in 1983.

Entertainment Software Association

601 Massachusetts Avenue NW, Suite 300

Washington, DC 20001

Email: esa@theESA.com

Website: http://www.theesa.com

Facebook: @TheEntertainmentSoftwareAssociation

Twitter: @theESA

The Entertainment Software Association is an advocacy and lobbying organization representing the interests of the gaming industry in Washington, DC, and other locations.

International Digital Media and Arts Association (iDMAa)

c/o School of Media Arts

Columbia College Chicago

33 E. Congress, Room 600B

Chicago, IL 60605

Email: admin@idmaa.org

Website: http://www.idmaa.org

The International Digital Media and Arts Association (iDMAa) is a collaboration among fifteen universities exploring new and changing opportunities, including educational development, in the area of digital media arts.

Internet Creators Guild

Facebook: @internetcreatorsguild

Twitter: @icguild

Website: https://internetcreatorsguild.com

The Internet Creators Guild bills itself as an organization set up to promote the interests of online content creators and make this new and growing profession sustainable.

YouTube

901 Cherry Avenue

San Bruno, CA 94066

(650) 253-0000

Website: http://www.youtube.com

Instagram and Twitter: @youtube

YouTube is the world's largest and most influential video-sharing platform, which provides amateurs and professionals alike the ability to post and make money from video content.

FOR FURTHER READING

Bernhardt, Carolyn. *Film It! YouTube Projects for the Real World.* Minneapolis, MN: Checkerboard Library/ABDO Publishing, 2017.

Centore, Michael. *YouTube and Videos of Everything!* Broomall, PA: Mason Crest, 2018.

Furgang, Adam. *20 Great Career-Building Activities Using YouTube.* New York, NY: Rosen Publishing, 2017.

Hall, Kevin. *Creating and Building Your Own YouTube Channel.* New York, NY: Rosen Publishing, 2017.

Juilly, Brett. *Make Your Own Amazing YouTube Videos: Learn How to Film, Edit, and Upload Quality Videos to YouTube.* New York, NY: Racehorse for Young Readers, 2017.

Klein, Emily. *From Me to YouTube: The Unofficial Guide to Bethany Mota.* New York, NY: Scholastic, 2015.

Mooney, Carla. *How the Internet Is Changing Society.* San Diego, CA: ReferencePoint Press, 2016.

Owings, Lisa. *YouTube.* New York, NY: Checkerboard Library/ABDO Publishing, 2017.

Scott, Cecilia. *YouTube: How Steve Chen Changed the Way We Watch Videos.* Broomall, PA: Mason Crest, 2015.

Wooster, Patricia. *YouTube Founders Steve Chen, Chad Hurley, and Jawed Karim.* Minneapolis, MN: Lerner Digital, 2018.

BIBLIOGRAPHY

Alexander, Julia. "Markiplier Doesn't Want People to Think YouTubers are 'Dancing Monkeys.'" Polygon.com, February 14, 2018. https://www.polygon.com/2018/2/14/17009050/markiplier -youtube-culture-twitch-logan-paul.

Ault, Susanne. "Digital Star Popularity Grows Versus Mainstream Celebrities." *Variety*, July 23, 2015. https://variety.com/2015 /digital/news/youtubers-teen-survey-ksi-pewdiepie-1201544882.

Dryden, Liam. "Markiplier Just Announced a Freakin' World Tour and Fans Are Losing It." We The Unicorns, September 6, 2017. https://www.wetheunicorns.com/news/markiplier-tour-world -youre-welcome.

Ell, Kellie. "Video Game Industry Is Booming with Continued Revenue." CNBC, July 18, 2018. https://www.cnbc .com/2018/07/18/video-game-industry-is-booming-with -continued-revenue.html.

Hernandez, Patricia. "Famous YouTubers Go on TV, Teach Jimmy Kimmel a Lesson." Kotaku.com, September 4, 2015. https:// kotaku.com/famous-youtubers-teach-jimmy-kimmel-a -lesson-1728678078.

Inside Edition. "YouTuber Markiplier Thanks Fans for Support After Niece's Death in Car Accident." June 29, 2018. https://www .insideedition.com/youtuber-markiplier-thanks-fans-support -after-nieces-death-car-accident-4463.

Lewis, Rebecca. "YouTuber Markiplier Reveals He Is Taking a Break After Niece Was Killed in Car Crash." *Metro*, June 28, 2018. https://metro.co.uk/2018/06/28/youtuber-markiplier -reveals-taking-break-niece-killed-car-crash-7668558.

Markiplier Transcripts. "Draw My Life." Retrieved September 28, 2018. http://markipliertranscripts.tumblr.com/post/80372689381/draw-my-life.

Martin, John. "Facts You May Not Know About Markiplier." Looper.com. Retrieved September 25, 2018. https://www.looper.com/33754/facts-may-know-markiplier.

McKinnon, Andrew. *YouTube: Ultimate YouTube Guide to Building a Channel, Audience, and to Start Making Passive Income*. North Charleston, SC: CreateSpace Independent, 2015.

O'Connor, Clare. "Forbes Top Influencers: Meet Markiplier, the Gamer Who Has Hollywood Calling." *Forbes* magazine, June 20, 2017. https://www.forbes.com/sites/clareoconnor/2017/06/20/forbes-top-influencers-markiplier-mark-fischbach-gaming-youtuber/#c6592ba38fd9.

Roberts, Bill. "How Much Does Markiplier Make? Monthly & Yearly YouTube Earnings Breakdown." Vlogger Gear, November 6, 2017. http://vloggergear.com/how-much-does-markiplier-make.

Schreier, Jason. "Banned from YouTube, These YouTubers Share Their Stories." Kotaku.com, December 3, 2012. https://kotaku.com/5964998/banned-from-making-money-these-youtubers-share-their-stories.

Index

About the Author

Philip Wolny is an author and editor hailing from Poland by way of Queens, New York. He has written numerous young-adult educational texts on technology and the internet, including *Google and You: Maximizing Your Google Experience, Andrew Mason and Groupon, Foursquare and Other Location-Based Services*, and *Creating Electronic Graphic Organizers*. He lives in New York City with his wife and daughter.

Photo Credits

Design and Layout: Brian Garvey; Editor: Siyavush Saidian; Photo Researcher: Nicole DiMella